PAINTED TURTLES

The Ultimate Owners Guide On Raising And Caring Of Painted Turtle For Beginners: Training, Feeding, Health, Reproduction, Housing And Much More

Mary Hook

Table of Contents

INTRODUCTION TO PAINTED TURTLES 2
    A. OVERVIEW OF PAINTED TURTLES 2
    B. IMPORTANCE OF PROPER CARE AND HABITAT 2
    C. PURPOSE OF THE BOOK 2
A. Overview of Painted Turtles: 2
B. Importance of Proper Care and Habitat: 5
C. Purpose of the Book: 7
CHAPTER ONE 10
UNDERSTANDING PAINTED TURTLES 10
    A. Species Overview 10
    B. Natural Habitat And Behavior 10
    C. Physical Characteristics 10
A. Species Overview: 10
B. Natural Habitat and Behavior: 12
C. Physical Characteristics: 14
CHAPTER TWO 16
SETTING UP THE HABITAT 16
    A. Tank Selection And Size Guidelines 16
    B. Substrate Options 16
    C. Heating And Lighting Requirements 16
    D. Water Quality And Filtration 16
B. Substrate Options: 17
C. Heating and Lighting Requirements: 18

D. Water Quality and Filtration: 20

FEEDING AND NUTRITION 22

   A. Dietary Needs Of Painted Turtles 22

   B. Types Of Food Suitable For Painted Turtles 22

   C. Feeding Schedule And Portion Control 22

   D. Calcium And Vitamin Supplementation 22

   A. Dietary Needs of Painted Turtles: 22

   B. Types of Food Suitable for Painted Turtles: 24

   C. Feeding Schedule and Portion Control: 25

   D. Calcium and Vitamin Supplementation: 27

CHAPTER THREE 29

HEALTH AND WELLNESS 29

   A. Common Health Issues In Painted Turtles 29

   B. Signs Of Illness And Injury 29

   C. Preventative Care Measures 29

   D. Veterinary Care And Finding A Reptile Vet 29

   A. Common Health Issues in Painted Turtles: 29

   B. Signs of Illness and Injury: 31

   C. Preventative Care Measures: 32

   D. Veterinary Care and Finding a Reptile Vet: 34

CHAPTER FOUR 36

HANDLING AND INTERACTION 36

   A. Proper Handling Techniques 36

   B. Socialization And Enrichment 36

C. Bonding With Your Painted Turtle 36
A. Proper Handling Techniques: 36
B. Socialization and Enrichment: 37
C. Bonding with Your Painted Turtle: 39
CHAPTER FIVE 41
BREEDING AND REPRODUCTION 41
A. Overview Of Painted Turtle Breeding Behavior 41
B. Preparing For Breeding 41
C. Incubating Eggs And Caring For Hatchlings 41
A. Overview of Painted Turtle Breeding Behavior: 41
B. Preparing for Breeding: 43
C. Incubating Eggs and Caring for Hatchlings: 45
CHAPTER SIX 47
LEGAL CONSIDERATIONS AND CONSERVATION 47
A. Legal Restrictions On Owning Painted Turtles 47
B. Ethical Considerations In Turtle Ownership 47
C. Conservation Efforts For Painted Turtles In The Wild 47
A. Legal Restrictions on Owning Painted Turtles: 47
B. Ethical Considerations in Turtle Ownership: 49
C. Conservation Efforts for Painted Turtles in the Wild: 50
FREQUENTLY ASKED QUESTIONS (FAQS) 53
A. Addressing Common Queries And Concerns 53
B. Troubleshooting Guide For Common Problems 53
A. Addressing Common Queries and Concerns: 53

CONCLUSION 59
   A. Recap Of Key Points 59
   B. Final Tips For Successful Painted Turtle Care 59
   C. Encouragement For Responsible Pet Ownership And Conservation Efforts 59
A. Recap of Key Points: 59
B. Final Tips for Successful Painted Turtle Care: 61
C. Encouragement for Responsible Pet Ownership and Conservation Efforts: 63
THE END 65

INTRODUCTION TO PAINTED TURTLES

A. OVERVIEW OF PAINTED TURTLES

B. IMPORTANCE OF PROPER CARE AND HABITAT

C. PURPOSE OF THE BOOK

A. Overview of Painted Turtles: Painted turtles are a species of freshwater turtles native to North America. They are known for their colorful shells, which often feature yellow, red, and olive-green markings. These turtles are popular pets due to their striking appearance and relatively small size compared to other turtle species.

Physical Characteristics: Painted turtles typically have a smooth, oval-shaped shell that measures around 4 to 10 inches in length. Their shells feature intricate patterns of yellow, red, and green stripes, giving them their distinctive appearance. Their skin is usually dark with red or yellow stripes, and they have webbed feet adapted for swimming.

Habitat and Distribution: Painted turtles are commonly found in shallow ponds, lakes, marshes, and slow-moving streams across North America, from southern Canada down to northern Mexico. They prefer habitats with plenty of aquatic vegetation and basking spots where they can regulate their body temperature.

Behavior and Diet: Painted turtles are primarily herbivores, feeding on a diet of aquatic plants, algae, and small invertebrates. They are often active during the day, basking in the sun to warm themselves. They are also capable swimmers and can often be seen basking on logs or rocks near the water's edge.

B. Importance of Proper Care and Habitat:

Proper care and habitat are essential for the health and well-being of painted turtles, whether they're kept as pets or observed in the wild. Here's why:

Temperature Regulation: Painted turtles are ectothermic, meaning they rely on external sources of heat to regulate their body temperature. In captivity, it's crucial to provide them with a basking area under a heat lamp where they can warm themselves. In the wild, they depend on access to sunlight for basking, so preserving their natural habitat with ample basking spots is important.

Water Quality: Painted turtles are highly dependent on clean, unpolluted water for survival. In captivity, their tank or enclosure should have a filtration system to maintain water quality. In the wild, conservation efforts are needed to protect their aquatic habitats from pollution and habitat destruction.

Nutrition: Providing a balanced diet is essential for the health of painted turtles. In captivity, this includes a combination of commercial turtle pellets, leafy greens, and occasional live or frozen prey items. In the wild, preserving their natural food sources and habitat ensures they have access to the nutrients they need to thrive.

C. Purpose of the Book:

The purpose of a book on painted turtles could vary depending on its intended audience and focus. However, some common purposes might include:

Educational Resource: The book may serve as an educational resource for turtle enthusiasts, pet owners, educators, and conservationists. It could provide comprehensive information on painted turtle biology, behavior, ecology, and conservation.

Care Guide: For pet owners, the book may offer practical guidance on caring for painted turtles in captivity. This could include advice on habitat setup, diet and nutrition, health care, and behavioral enrichment.

Conservation Advocacy: The book may also raise awareness about the conservation challenges facing painted turtles and other freshwater turtle species. It could highlight the importance of habitat preservation, pollution reduction, and responsible pet ownership to ensure the long-term survival of these iconic reptiles.

CHAPTER ONE

UNDERSTANDING PAINTED TURTLES

A. Species Overview

B. Natural Habitat And Behavior

C. Physical Characteristics

A. Species Overview:

Painted turtles (Chrysemys picta) are a species of freshwater turtle native to North America. They belong to the family Emydidae, which includes pond turtles and marsh turtles. Painted turtles are known for their vibrant shell patterns and are popular among turtle enthusiasts. There are four recognized subspecies of painted turtles:

Eastern Painted Turtle (Chrysemys picta picta): Found in eastern North America, from southern Canada to the Gulf of Mexico.

Midland Painted Turtle (Chrysemys picta marginata): Distributed across the Great Lakes region and surrounding areas.

Southern Painted Turtle (Chrysemys picta dorsalis): Inhabits the southeastern United States.

Western Painted Turtle (Chrysemys picta bellii): Found in the western United States and parts of Canada.

Painted turtles are characterized by their colorful shell patterns, which often include yellow, red, and olive-green markings. They have a relatively small size compared to other turtle species, with adults typically measuring between 4 to 10 inches in length.

B. Natural Habitat and Behavior:
Habitat: Painted turtles inhabit various freshwater habitats, including ponds, lakes, marshes, rivers, and streams. They prefer shallow waters with ample vegetation and basking spots. Painted turtles are commonly found basking on

logs, rocks, or emergent vegetation near the water's edge.

Behavior: Painted turtles are diurnal, meaning they are active during the day. They spend much of their time basking in the sun to regulate their body temperature. Painted turtles are also capable swimmers and often forage for food underwater. During the colder months, they may hibernate at the bottom of bodies of water or in mud.

Diet: Painted turtles are omnivores, although they tend to have a primarily herbivorous diet. They feed on a variety of aquatic plants, algae, and small invertebrates such as insects, crustaceans, and mollusks. In captivity, they can be fed a diet consisting of commercial turtle pellets, leafy greens, and occasional protein sources.

C. Physical Characteristics:

Shell: Painted turtles have a smooth, oval-shaped shell known as a carapace. The shell typically ranges from dark olive-green to black and features intricate patterns of red, yellow, and orange markings. The shell provides protection for the turtle's body and internal organs.

Skin: The skin of painted turtles is typically dark-colored with red or yellow stripes running along their limbs and neck. Their skin is relatively smooth and covered in scales.

Limbs and Feet: Painted turtles have four webbed feet adapted for swimming. Their limbs are typically dark-colored with lighter stripes or markings.

CHAPTER TWO

SETTING UP THE HABITAT

A. Tank Selection And Size Guidelines

B. Substrate Options

C. Heating And Lighting Requirements

D. Water Quality And Filtration

A. Tank Selection and Size Guidelines:

Tank Size: The size of the tank depends on the size and number of turtles you plan to keep. As a general guideline, a single adult painted turtle requires a tank with a minimum size of 40 gallons. For every additional turtle, add 10-20 gallons per turtle to accommodate their space needs adequately.

Aquarium Type: Opt for a glass or acrylic aquarium with a secure lid to prevent escapes. A tank with a long footprint rather than a tall one is preferable, as it provides more swimming space and surface area for basking.

B. Substrate Options:

Substrate: Choose a substrate that is safe for turtles and easy to clean. Options include smooth gravel, river rocks, or large pebbles. Avoid substrates that are small enough to be ingested by the turtle, as this can lead to digestive issues.

Bare Bottom Tanks: Some turtle owners prefer to keep the tank bottom bare to make cleaning easier. This is especially common in larger tanks with powerful filtration systems.

C. Heating and Lighting Requirements:

Basking Area: Painted turtles require a basking area where they can climb out of the water and dry off completely. This area should be large enough to accommodate all turtles in the tank simultaneously and should include a flat platform or floating basking dock.

Heat Lamp: Provide a heat lamp over the basking area to create a warm basking spot with temperatures ranging from 85-90°F (29-32°C). Use a ceramic heat emitter or a halogen bulb to generate heat without emitting light at night.

UVB Lighting: Painted turtles require UVB lighting to metabolize calcium and prevent metabolic bone disease. Use a fluorescent UVB bulb specifically designed for reptiles and replaces it every 6-12 months, as UVB output diminishes over time.

D. Water Quality and Filtration:
Filtration System: Invest in a high-quality filtration system capable of handling the tank's water volume and keeping it clean. A combination of mechanical, biological, and chemical filtration is ideal for maintaining water quality.

Water Heater: Maintain the water temperature between 75-80°F (24-27°C) using a submersible aquarium heater. This ensures that the turtles remain comfortable and active.

Water Depth: Provide a water depth of at least twice the length of the turtle's shell to allow for swimming and diving. Ensure that the water is not too deep for juvenile turtles to reach the surface for breathing.

FEEDING AND NUTRITION

A. Dietary Needs Of Painted Turtles

B. Types Of Food Suitable For Painted Turtles

C. Feeding Schedule And Portion Control

D. Calcium And Vitamin Supplementation

A. Dietary Needs of Painted Turtles:

Omnivorous Diet: Painted turtles are omnivores, meaning they consume both plant and animal matter. A balanced diet is essential to meet their nutritional requirements and maintain their health.

Variety: Offer a variety of foods to ensure your turtle receives all the essential nutrients. This includes plant matter, such as leafy greens and vegetables, as well as animal protein sources like insects, fish, and crustaceans.

Calcium: Painted turtles require calcium for proper shell and bone development. Ensure that their diet includes calcium-rich foods or supplements to prevent metabolic bone disease.

B. Types of Food Suitable for Painted Turtles:

Plant Matter: Offer a variety of leafy greens and vegetables, such as kale, collard greens, romaine lettuce, dandelion greens, carrots, and squash. These provide essential vitamins, minerals, and fiber.

Protein Sources: Provide animal protein sources, including live or frozen insects (such as crickets, mealworms, and earthworms), fish (such as feeder fish or small pieces of cooked fish), shrimp, and commercial turtle pellets or sticks.

Commercial Diets: High-quality commercial turtle pellets or sticks formulated specifically for aquatic turtles can be a convenient option to ensure balanced nutrition. Look for brands that contain a mix of plant-based and animal-based ingredients.

C. Feeding Schedule and Portion Control:

Frequency: Feed adult painted turtles 3-4 times per week, offering a variety of foods at each feeding session. Juvenile turtles may require more frequent feedings, up to once daily, to support their growth and development.

Portion Control: Offer food portions that are appropriate for the size and age of your turtle. Avoid overfeeding, as obesity can lead to health issues. Monitor your turtle's body condition and adjust portion sizes accordingly.

Feeding Time: Feed your turtles during daylight hours when they are most active and likely to eat. Remove any uneaten food after 15-20 minutes to prevent water contamination.

D. Calcium and Vitamin Supplementation:

Calcium Supplement: Dust calcium powder onto your turtle's food several times a week to ensure they receive adequate calcium. This is especially important for growing turtles and females during egg-laying periods.

Vitamin Supplement: Provide a multivitamin supplement containing vitamins A, D3, and E once or twice a week to help meet your turtle's nutritional needs. Follow the manufacturer's dosage recommendations carefully.

Natural Sunlight: Whenever possible, allow your turtles to bask in natural sunlight. UVB radiation from sunlight helps turtles synthesize vitamin D3, essential for calcium absorption and overall health.

CHAPTER THREE

HEALTH AND WELLNESS

A. Common Health Issues In Painted Turtles

B. Signs Of Illness And Injury

C. Preventative Care Measures

D. Veterinary Care And Finding A Reptile Vet

A. Common Health Issues in Painted Turtles:

Shell Rot: Shell rot is a common bacterial infection that affects the shell of turtles, often caused by poor water quality or injuries. Symptoms include soft spots, discoloration, and foul odor on the shell.

Respiratory Infections: Respiratory infections can occur due to inadequate basking temperatures, poor water quality, or stress. Symptoms include wheezing, gasping for air, nasal discharge, and lethargy.

Metabolic Bone Disease (MBD): MBD is a condition caused by calcium and vitamin D3 deficiencies, resulting in weakened bones and shell deformities. Symptoms include soft or misshapen shells, swollen limbs, and difficulty walking.

Parasites: Internal and external parasites, such as worms, ticks, and mites, can affect painted turtles. Symptoms may include weight loss, lethargy, diarrhea, and visible parasites on the skin or shell.

B. Signs of Illness and Injury:
Changes in Appetite: Decreased or loss of appetite can indicate underlying health issues.

Abnormal Behavior: Lethargy, excessive basking, or hiding may signal illness or discomfort.

Physical Symptoms: Look for signs of shell damage, discoloration, lesions, swelling, or abnormal growths.

Respiratory Signs: Wheezing, gasping for air, nasal discharge, or bubbling at the nostrils may indicate respiratory issues.

Changes in Stool: Diarrhea, blood in the stool, or changes in stool color or consistency may indicate digestive problems.

C. Preventative Care Measures:
Maintain Clean Water: Regularly clean and maintain the turtle's habitat to prevent bacterial growth and maintain water quality.

Provide Proper Nutrition: Offer a balanced diet consisting of a variety of foods to ensure adequate nutrition and prevent deficiencies.

Monitor Temperature and Lighting: Maintain appropriate basking temperatures and UVB lighting to support thermoregulation and vitamin synthesis.

Handle with Care: Handle your turtle gently and avoid dropping or mishandling, which can lead to injuries.

Regular Health Checks: Monitor your turtle's behavior, appetite, and physical condition regularly to detect any changes early.

D. Veterinary Care and Finding a Reptile Vet:

Find a Reptile Veterinarian: Locate a qualified reptile veterinarian experienced in treating turtles. You can ask for recommendations from local reptile clubs, breeders, or online reptile communities.

Schedule Regular Check-ups: Schedule annual wellness exams with a reptile vet to assess your turtle's health and address any concerns.

Emergency Care: In case of sudden illness or injury, seek immediate veterinary attention. Have the contact information of a reptile vet or emergency clinic readily available.

CHAPTER FOUR

HANDLING AND INTERACTION

A. Proper Handling Techniques

B. Socialization And Enrichment

C. Bonding With Your Painted Turtle

A. Proper Handling Techniques:
Wash Hands: Before handling your turtle, wash your hands thoroughly with soap and water to remove any potential contaminants.

Handle Gently: When picking up your turtle, support its body properly with both hands. Avoid grabbing or squeezing the turtle, as this can cause stress or injury.

Avoid Dropping: Be cautious when handling your turtle to prevent accidental drops or falls, which can injure the turtle.

Limit Handling: While it's important for turtles to get accustomed to human interaction, limit handling to short periods to minimize stress. Over handling can cause stress and disrupt the turtle's natural behaviors.

B. Socialization and Enrichment:
Provide Enrichment: Offer a variety of enrichment activities, such as introducing new objects or rearranging

the habitat, to stimulate your turtle's mind and encourage natural behaviors.

Interaction with Environment: Allow your turtle to explore its environment and interact with different elements, such as plants, rocks, and basking spots.

Safe Encounters: Supervise interactions with other pets or household members to ensure the safety of both the turtle and others. Keep other animals, such as dogs or cats, away from the turtle to prevent stress or injury.

C. Bonding with Your Painted Turtle:

Respect Boundaries: Understand that turtles may not seek out interaction or affection in the same way as other pets. Respect your turtle's boundaries and allow it to retreat to its hiding spots when it feels threatened or stressed.

Consistent Presence: Spend time near the turtle's habitat regularly to become familiar to it. Turtles may become more comfortable with your presence over time.

Offer Treats: Associate positive experiences with your presence by offering occasional treats, such as small pieces of their favorite food, during interactions.

Observe Behaviors: Pay attention to your turtle's body language and behaviors to gauge its comfort level. If the turtle seems relaxed and active in your presence, it may be more receptive to interaction.

CHAPTER FIVE

BREEDING AND REPRODUCTION

A. Overview Of Painted Turtle Breeding Behavior

B. Preparing For Breeding

C. Incubating Eggs And Caring For Hatchlings

A. Overview of Painted Turtle Breeding Behavior:

Courtship: Breeding behavior typically begins in the spring when water temperatures rise. Male painted turtles may engage in courtship displays to attract females, which can include swimming around them, bobbing their heads, and gently biting their shells or limbs.

Mating: Once a female has been courted, mating occurs in the water. The male mounts the female from behind and clasps onto her shell with his claws, aligning their cloacas for fertilization.

Nesting: After mating, the female seeks out a suitable nesting site on land, typically in sandy or loose soil. She digs a nest cavity using her hind limbs and lays her eggs in the nest.

Egg Deposition: The female deposits her eggs one by one into the nest cavity, covering them with soil afterward. A typical clutch size for painted turtles ranges from 4 to 20 eggs, depending on the species and age of the female.

B. Preparing for Breeding:
Habitat Conditions: Ensure that the breeding pair is housed in a spacious and suitable habitat with access to both land and water areas. Provide basking spots, hiding places, and ample space for courtship and nesting behaviors.

Temperature and Lighting: Maintain appropriate temperature and lighting conditions to mimic seasonal changes and stimulate breeding behavior. Gradually increase water temperatures in the spring to trigger mating and nesting instincts.

Healthy Diet: Provide a nutritious diet rich in calcium and vitamins to support reproductive health in both male and female turtles. A well-balanced diet helps ensure optimal egg development and fertility.

C. Incubating Eggs and Caring for Hatchlings:

Egg Incubation: After laying her eggs, the female covers the nest cavity and leaves the eggs to incubate naturally. Alternatively, you can collect the eggs and incubate them artificially in a controlled environment to improve hatch rates and survival.

Incubation Conditions: Maintain a stable temperature and humidity level in the incubator to promote healthy development of the embryos. The temperature should typically range between 78-85°F (25-29°C), depending on the species.

Hatchling Care: Once the eggs hatch, carefully remove the hatchlings from the incubator and place them in a shallow container with clean water. Provide a basking area and monitor their health closely during the first few weeks of life.

Feeding: Offer newly hatched turtles a diet of small, nutrient-rich foods such as commercial turtle hatchling pellets, small insects, and finely chopped vegetables. Ensure that they have access to clean water for swimming and hydration.

CHAPTER SIX

LEGAL CONSIDERATIONS AND CONSERVATION

A. Legal Restrictions On Owning Painted Turtles

B. Ethical Considerations In Turtle Ownership

C. Conservation Efforts For Painted Turtles In The Wild

A. Legal Restrictions on Owning Painted Turtles:

Wild Collection: Many regions have regulations governing the collection and possession of wild-caught painted turtles. In some areas, it may be illegal to capture or keep painted turtles from the wild without proper permits or licenses.

Species-specific Regulations: Some states or countries have specific laws and regulations regarding the ownership of painted turtles, including size limits, possession limits, and restrictions on selling or trading turtles.

Invasive Species Laws: In regions where painted turtles are not native, there may be restrictions on owning them as pets to prevent them from becoming invasive species and disrupting local ecosystems.

B. Ethical Considerations in Turtle Ownership:

Responsible Ownership: Responsible turtle ownership involves providing proper care, habitat, and nutrition to meet the turtle's physical and behavioral needs.

Avoiding Wild Capture: Whenever possible, acquire turtles from reputable breeders or rescue organizations rather than capturing them from the wild. Wild-caught turtles can suffer from stress, injuries, and diseases, and their removal can impact wild populations.

Education and Awareness: Educate yourself about the needs and behaviors of painted turtles to ensure you can provide them with a suitable and enriching environment. Share your knowledge with others to promote responsible turtle ownership and conservation efforts.

C. Conservation Efforts for Painted Turtles in the Wild:

Habitat Preservation: Protecting and restoring natural habitats, including wetlands, ponds, and waterways, is essential for maintaining healthy painted turtle populations.

Conservation efforts focus on preserving these habitats from pollution, habitat destruction, and human encroachment.

Research and Monitoring: Conducting research on painted turtle populations helps scientists understand their biology, ecology, and conservation needs. Monitoring programs track population trends, distribution, and threats to inform conservation strategies.

Legislative Protection: Advocacy efforts aim to enact and enforce laws and regulations that protect painted turtles and their habitats from exploitation, habitat loss, and other threats. This includes designating protected areas, implementing fishing regulations, and controlling pollution.

Community Engagement: Engaging local communities, stakeholders, and volunteers in conservation initiatives raises awareness about the importance of painted turtles and encourages participation in habitat restoration, monitoring, and education programs.

FREQUENTLY ASKED QUESTIONS (FAQS)

A. Addressing Common Queries And Concerns

B. Troubleshooting Guide For Common Problems

A. Addressing Common Queries and Concerns:

Q: What size tank do I need for my painted turtle?

A: Painted turtles require a tank with a minimum size of 40 gallons for a single adult turtle. Larger tanks are recommended for multiple turtles to provide ample swimming and basking space.

Q: What should I feed my painted turtle?

A: Painted turtles are omnivores and should be fed a balanced diet consisting of commercial turtle pellets, leafy greens, vegetables, and occasional protein sources like insects, fish, and crustaceans.

Q: How often should I clean my turtle's tank?

A: Regular tank maintenance is essential to maintain water quality. Perform partial water changes and clean the tank substrate and decorations weekly, and clean the filter monthly.

Q: How can I tell if my turtle is sick?

A: Signs of illness in turtles include decreased appetite, lethargy, abnormal behavior, shell abnormalities, respiratory issues, and changes in stool or urine color. If you notice any of these signs, consult a reptile veterinarian.

Q: Can I handle my painted turtle?

A: Painted turtles can be handled occasionally but should be handled gently and with care to avoid stress or injury. Limit handling to short periods and always support the turtle's body properly.

B. Troubleshooting Guide for Common Problems:

Problem: Foul odor in the tank

Solution: Check water quality parameters and perform a partial water change. Ensure that the filter is clean and functioning properly. Remove any uneaten food or waste from the tank.

Problem: Turtle not basking

Solution: Check the temperature and lighting in the basking area to ensure they are within the appropriate range. Provide a variety of basking spots with different temperatures and textures to encourage basking behavior.

Problem: Shell damage or abnormalities

Solution: Inspect the turtle's shell for signs of injury or shell rot. Ensure that the tank environment is clean and properly maintained to prevent shell issues. Consult a reptile veterinarian for treatment if needed.

Problem: Turtle not eating

Solution: Review the turtle's diet and ensure it is receiving a variety of nutritious foods. Check environmental conditions, such as water temperature and lighting, as these can affect appetite. If the issue persists, consult a veterinarian.

Problem: Cloudy or murky water

Solution: Test water quality parameters such as pH, ammonia, nitrite, and nitrate levels. Perform a partial water change to improve water clarity and maintain proper filtration to remove debris and waste.

CONCLUSION

A. Recap Of Key Points

B. Final Tips For Successful Painted Turtle Care

C. Encouragement For Responsible Pet Ownership And Conservation Efforts

A. Recap of Key Points:
Painted turtles are a species of freshwater turtle native to North America, known for their colorful shell patterns and popularity as pets.

Proper care and habitat are essential for painted turtles, including providing adequate space, water quality, heating, lighting, and a balanced diet.

Understanding the species' natural behaviors, such as basking, swimming, and feeding, helps ensure their well-being in captivity.

Breeding and reproduction in painted turtles require specific conditions and preparation to support successful mating, nesting, incubation, and hatchling care.

Legal considerations, ethical concerns, and conservation efforts play vital roles in responsible turtle ownership and protection of painted turtles in the wild.

B. Final Tips for Successful Painted Turtle Care:

Regularly monitor water quality parameters such as temperature, pH, ammonia, and nitrite levels to ensure a clean and healthy environment.

Offer a variety of foods to meet the nutritional needs of painted turtles, including commercial pellets, leafy greens, vegetables, and occasional protein sources.

Provide enrichment and stimulation through habitat features, such as basking spots, hiding places, and objects to explore.

Handle painted turtles gently and with care, avoiding excessive stress or mishandling.

Stay informed about local laws and regulations regarding turtle ownership and conservation efforts, and actively support initiatives to protect painted turtles and their habitats.

C. Encouragement for Responsible Pet Ownership and Conservation Efforts:

Responsible pet ownership involves providing proper care, attention, and respect for the needs and well-being of painted turtles and other pets.

Take proactive steps to minimize the impact of turtle ownership on wild populations, such as avoiding wild capture and supporting conservation initiatives.

Educate others about the importance of responsible pet ownership, conservation efforts, and the significance of preserving natural habitats for painted turtles and other wildlife.

THE END

Made in the USA
Monee, IL
30 June 2024